Flying Solo Violin

Unaccompanied

folk and fiddle fantasias

for playing your violin anywhere

Book Two

Myanna Harvey

Grateful thanks to Madi Lush for her help in preparing this manuscript!

Front Cover Image: Science, Industry and Business Library: General Collection , The New York Public Library. "Estampe anglaise de 1843 représentant l'aèroplane d'Henson dans un vol supposé aux environs de Londres." The New York Public Library Digital Collections. 1922. https://digitalcollections.nypl.org/items/627e815a-d992-c1e5-e040-e00a18062370

A note about metronome markings: The tempo markings are suggestions only. These pieces may be learned and played at any tempo the player chooses. For the faster solos, there is no speed limit!

CHP403

www.charveypublications.com - print books
www.learnstrings.com - PDF downloadable books
www.harveystringarrangements.com - chamber music

Flying Solo Violin, Book Two

all tunes arranged by Myanna Harvey

Table of Contents

	Title	Page
1.	**Haste to the Wedding** (Traditional)	2
2.	**Arirang** (Traditional)	4
3.	**Scarborough Fair** (Traditional)	6
4.	**Shenandoah** (Traditional)	8
5.	**Congress Reel** (Traditional)	10
6.	**Mary Hamilton** (Traditional)	12
7.	**Lord Garrick** (Traditional)	14
8.	**Kerry Dancing** (Traditional)	16
9.	**Wild Mountain Thyme** (Traditional)	18
10.	**President Garfield** (Traditional)	20
11.	**Danny Boy** (Traditional)	22
12.	**Aiken Drum** (Traditional)	24
13.	**Salley Gardens** (Traditional)	26
14.	**Coleraine** (Traditional)	28
15.	**After the Battle of Aughrim** (Traditional)	30
16.	**The Last Rose of Summer** (Traditional)	32
17.	**Roumanian Hora** (Traditional)	34
18.	**Waltzing Matilda** (Traditional)	36
19.	**Morrison's Jig** (Traditional)	38
20.	**Irish Air** (Traditional)	40
21.	**Peace Like a River** (Traditional)	42
22.	**Dark Eyes** (Hermann)	44

Flying Solo Violin, Book Two

41
46
51
56
61
mf
66
f
72
mp
78
ff

Arirang

Trad., arr. M. Harvey

42
47
52
56
mf
60
64
(3)
f
68
72
mp

♩=112-132
Scarborough Fair
Trad., arr. M. Harvey
Wistfully
mp
mf
f

45
4
f
50
V
56
V
4
61
V

Shenandoah
♩=100-116
Trad., arr. M. Harvey
Flowing
mf
5
mf
9
13
f
17
21
25
mf
29
f

33
37
41
45
mf
50
poco rit.
mp

Congress Reel
♩=176-208
Lively
Trad., arr. M. Harvey
mp
f
6
11
16
mf
21
26
0
0
31
ff
36
4

41
mp
46
50
f
55
59
63
ff
68
73
p
77
ff

Mary Hamilton

Trad., arr. M. Harvey

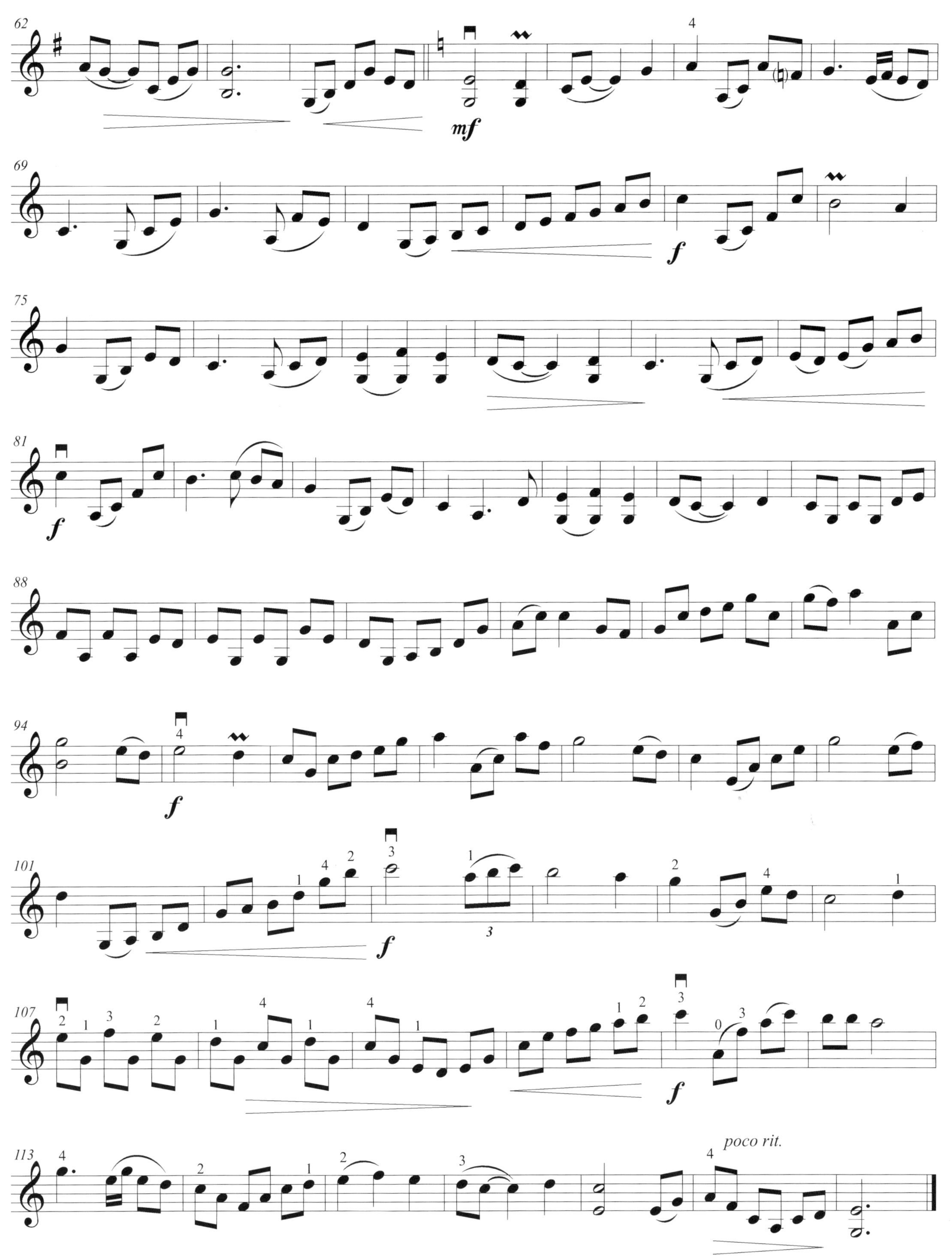
mf
f
f
f
f
f
poco rit.

Lord Garrick
♩= 96-116
Trad., arr. M. Harvey
Lively

25
28
31
34
37
40
mp
ff
f

Kerry Dancing
= 69-80
Trad., arr. M. Harvey
Moderately
mf
f
mf
f
mf
mp

poco rall.

Wild Mountain Thyme
♩ = 108-120
Trad., arr. M. Harvey
Poignantly
mf
f
mf
f

41
46
51
mf
56
61
f
66
71
75
poco rit.

President Garfield
♩= 88-108
Trad., arr. M. Harvey
Lively
mf
f
mf
f

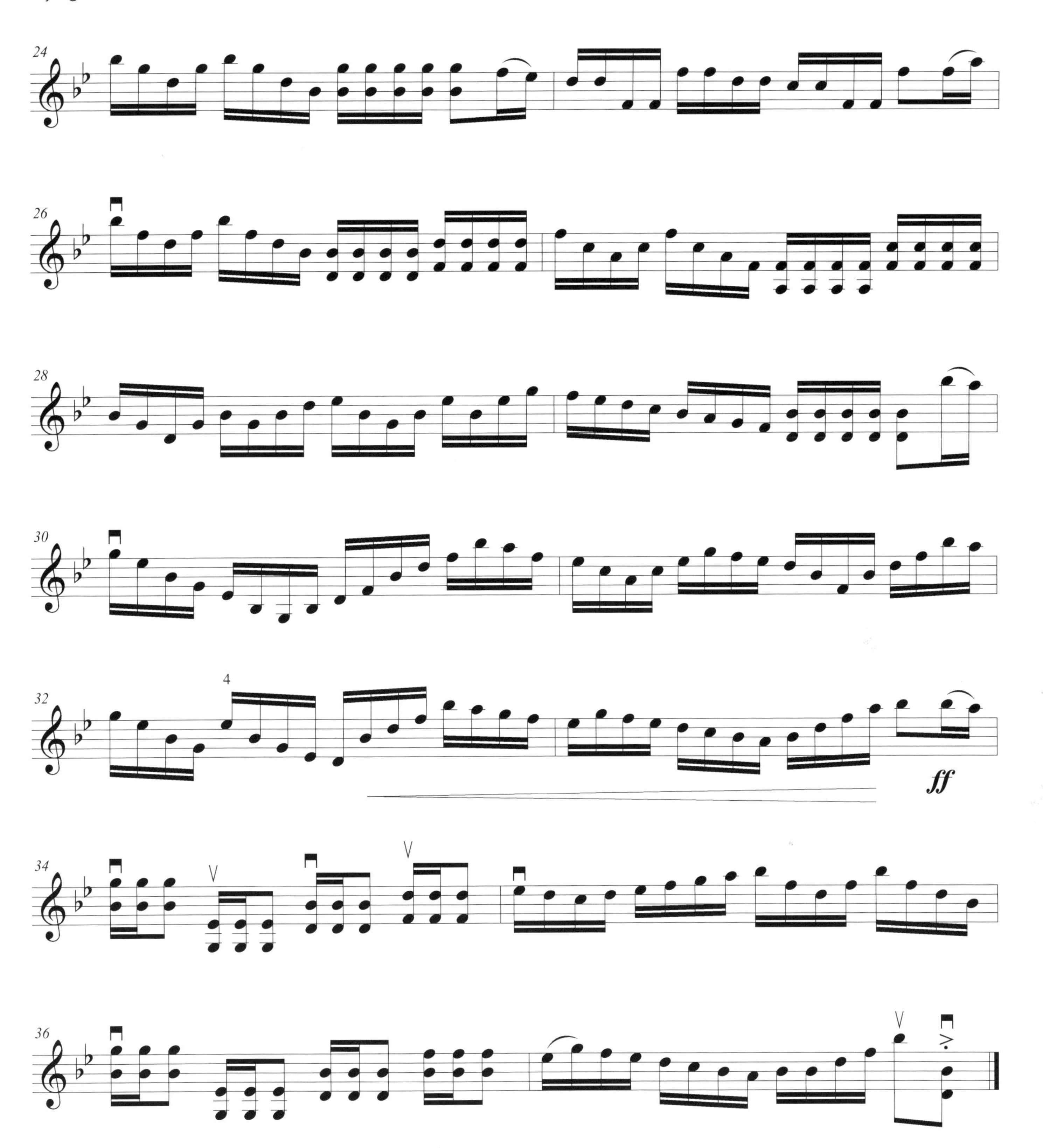
24
26
28
30
32
4
ff
34
36

Danny Boy
♩= 108-120
Trad., arr. M. Harvey
Poignantly
mf
mp
mf
f
mp
mf

46
51
56
61
66
71
76
80
f
mf
mp

Aiken Drum
♩.= 108-132
Lively
Trad., arr. M. Harvey
mf
mf
7
13
f
19
f
25
31
37
0 0
43
4
f
49
f

Salley Gardens
♩= 80-92
Trad., arr. M. Harvey
Flowing

mf
f
mf
poco rit.

Coleraine

Trad., arr. M. Harvey

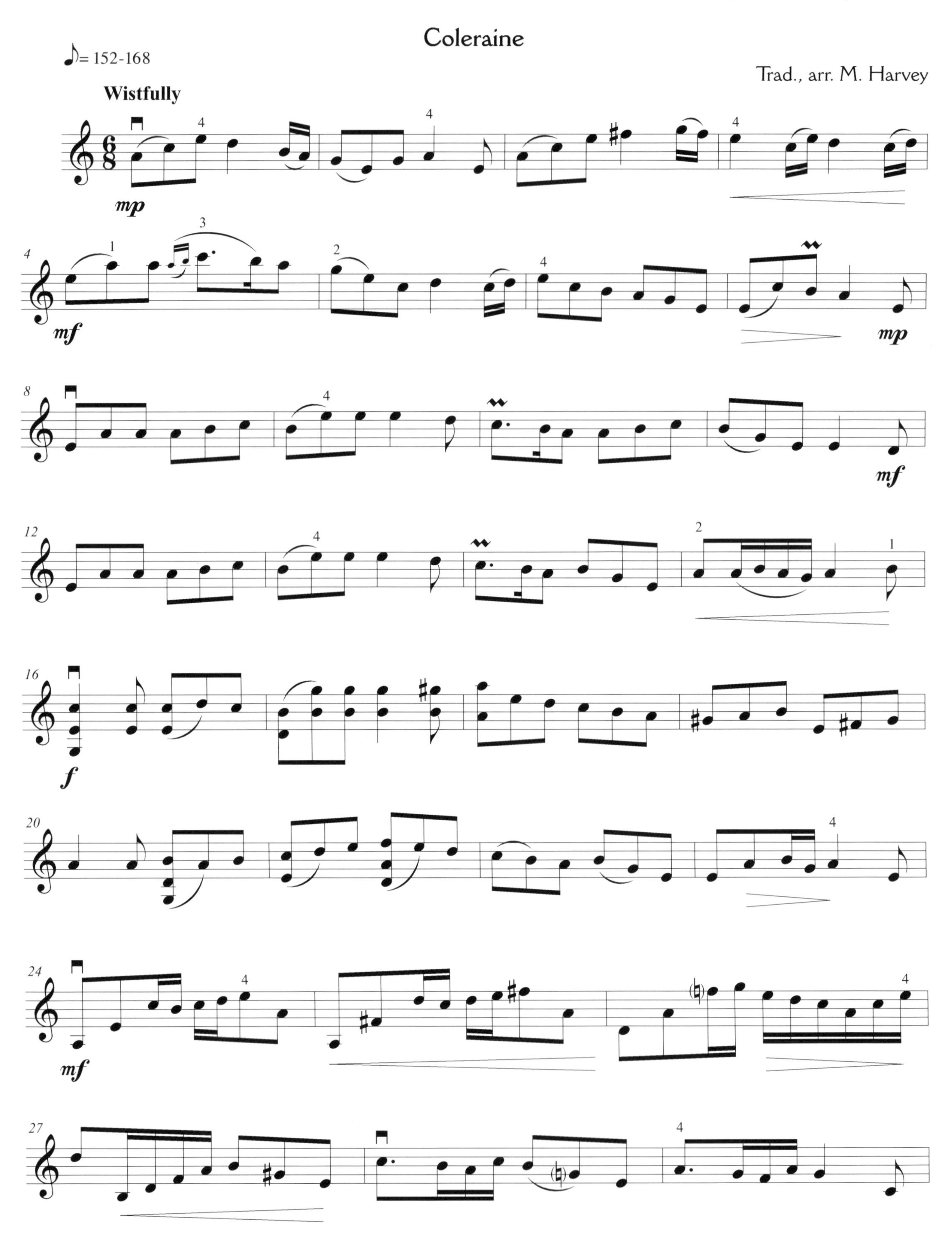

poco rit.

After the Battle of Aughrim
♩= 96-116
Trad., arr. M. Harvey
Lively

ff
fp
mf
f
mp
ff

The Last Rose of Summer

mf
f
mf
f
mf
f
ff
f
poco rall.

♩= 96-120
Lively
Roumanian Hora
Trad., arr. M. Harvey

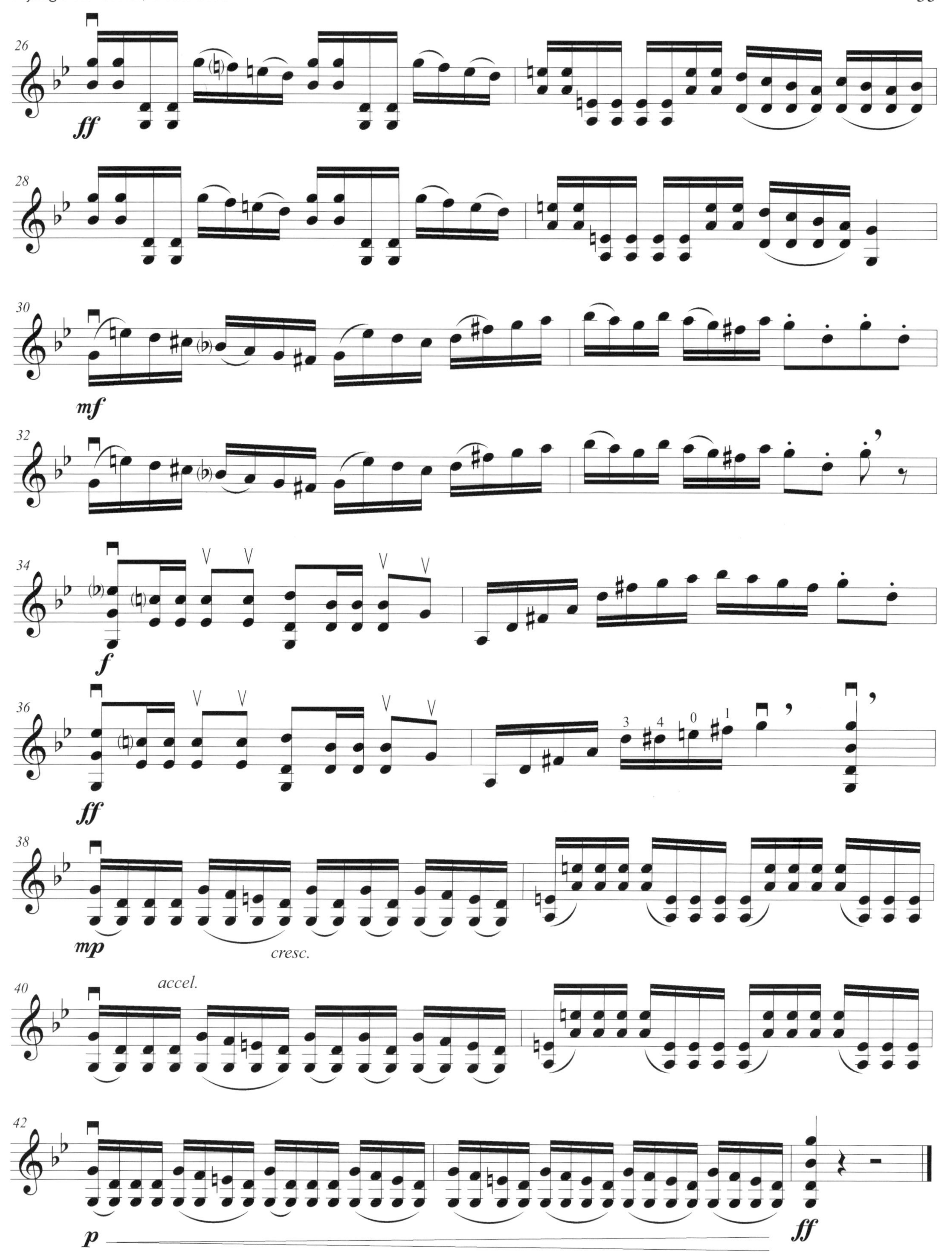
26
ff
28
30
mf
32
34
f
36
ff
3
4
0
1
38
mp
cresc.
40
accel.
42
p
ff

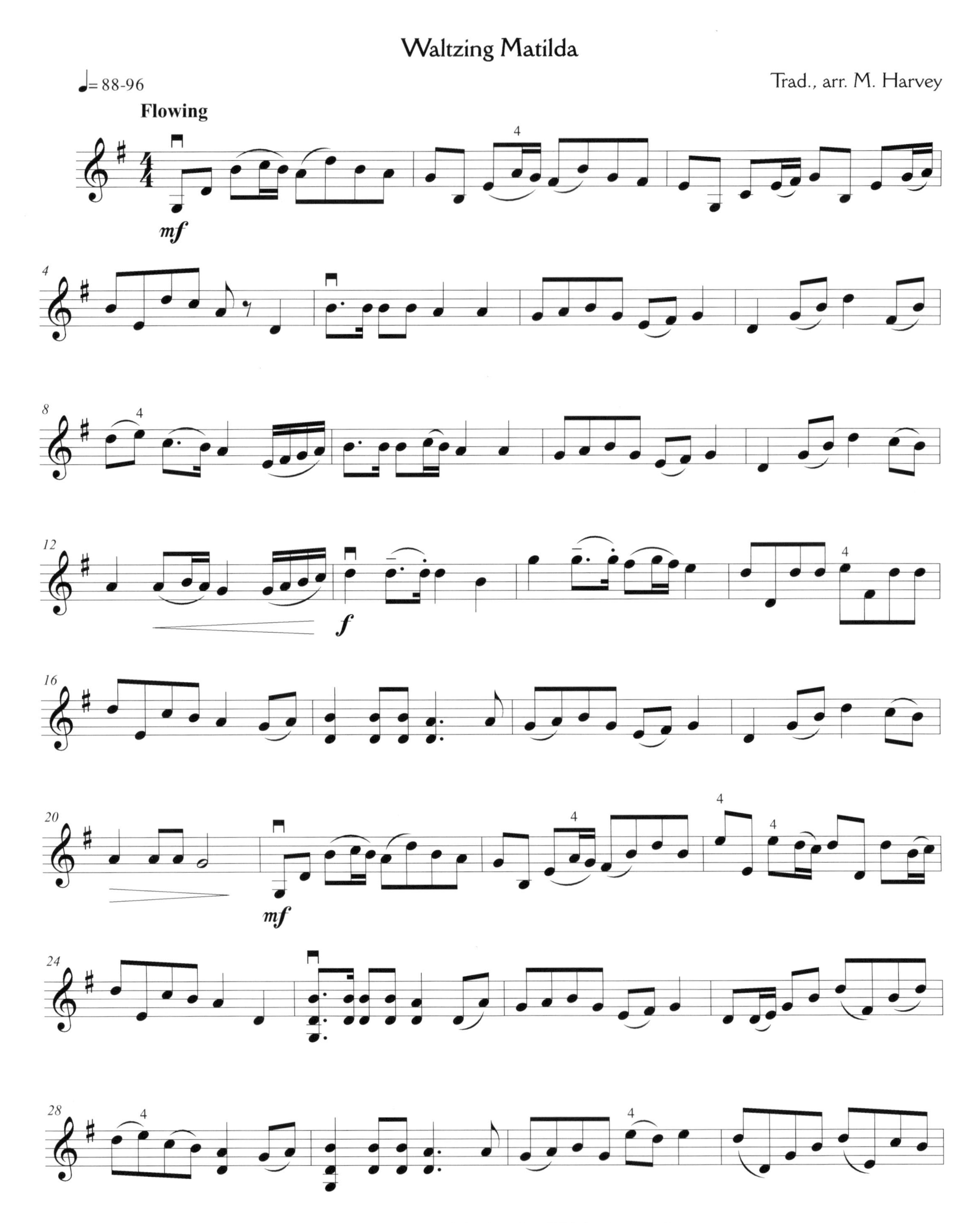
Waltzing Matilda
♩= 88-96
Trad., arr. M. Harvey
Flowing
mf
f
mf

poco rit.

Morrison's Jig

Trad., arr. M. Harvey

Irish Air

Trad., arr. M. Harvey

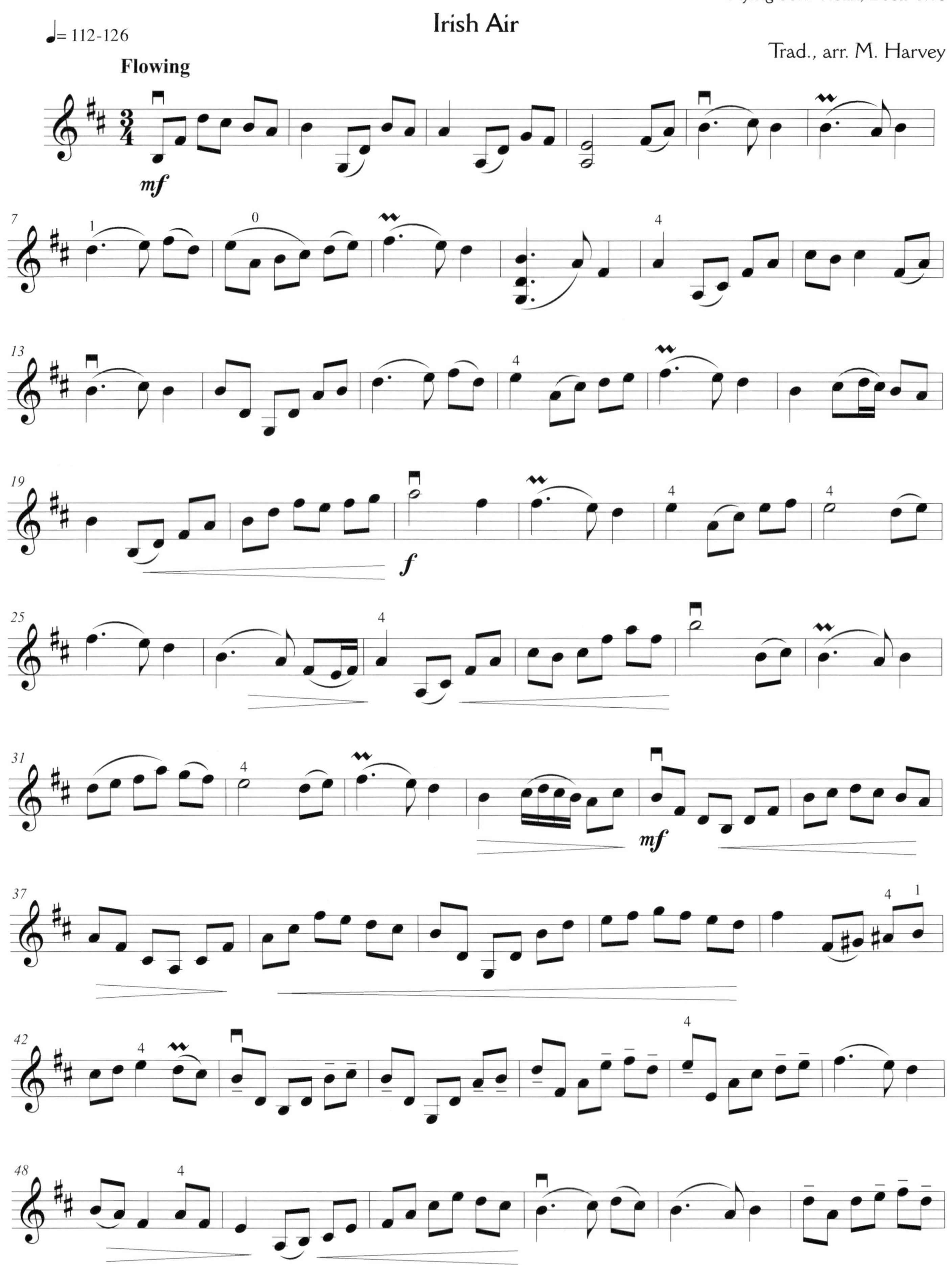

mp
f
poco rit.

Peace Like a River
♩= 120-126
With a Gentle Swing
Trad., arr. M. Harvey
mf
cresc.
f
mf

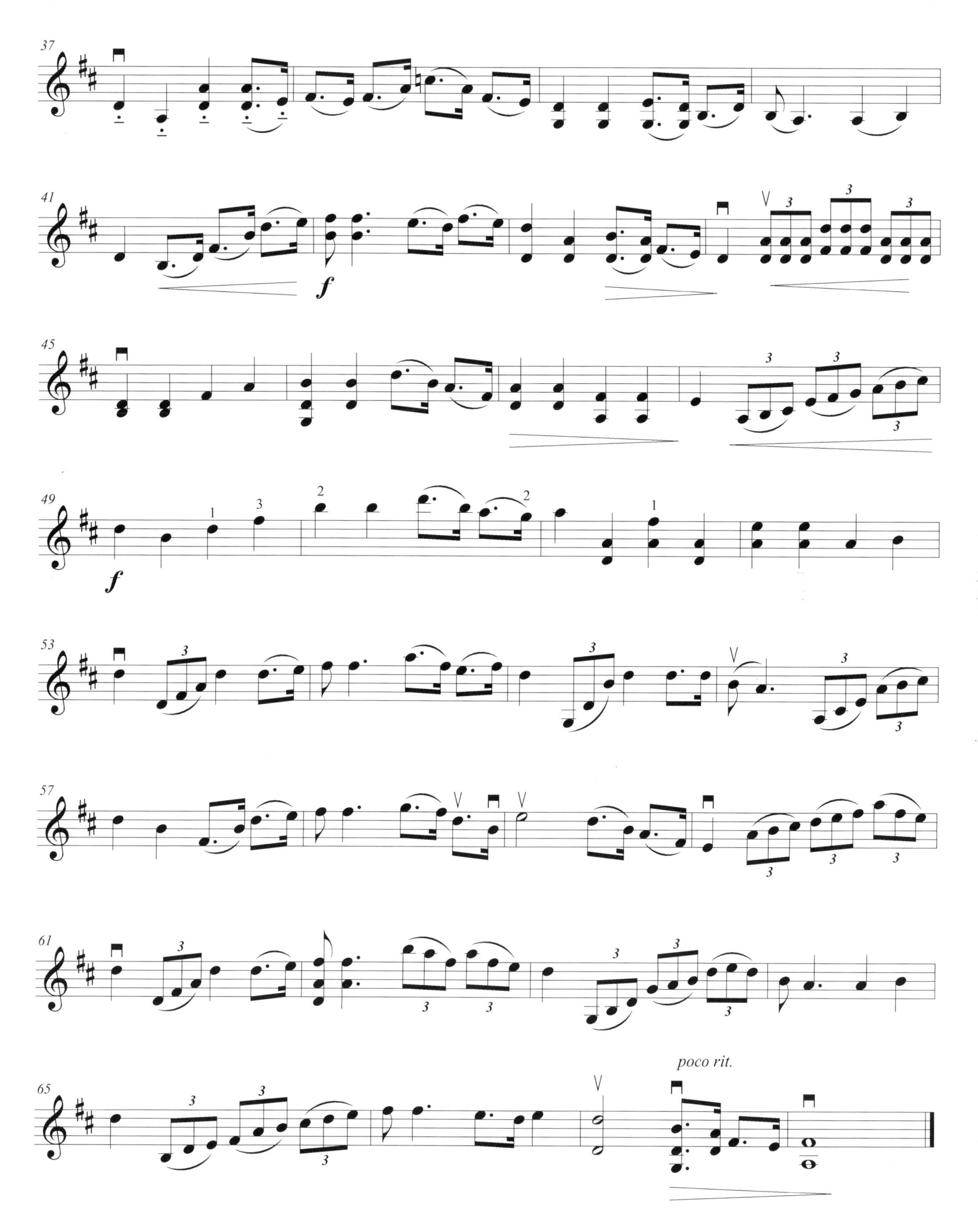
poco rit.

Dark Eyes

Freely, with Passion
Hermann, arr. M. Harvey
♩= 72
Allegro ♩= 120-132
cresc.

rubato
accel.
cresc.

You Might Also Like:

Fiddles on the Bandstand: Fun Duets for Two Violins Book One

all duets arranged by Myanna Harvey

Table of Contents

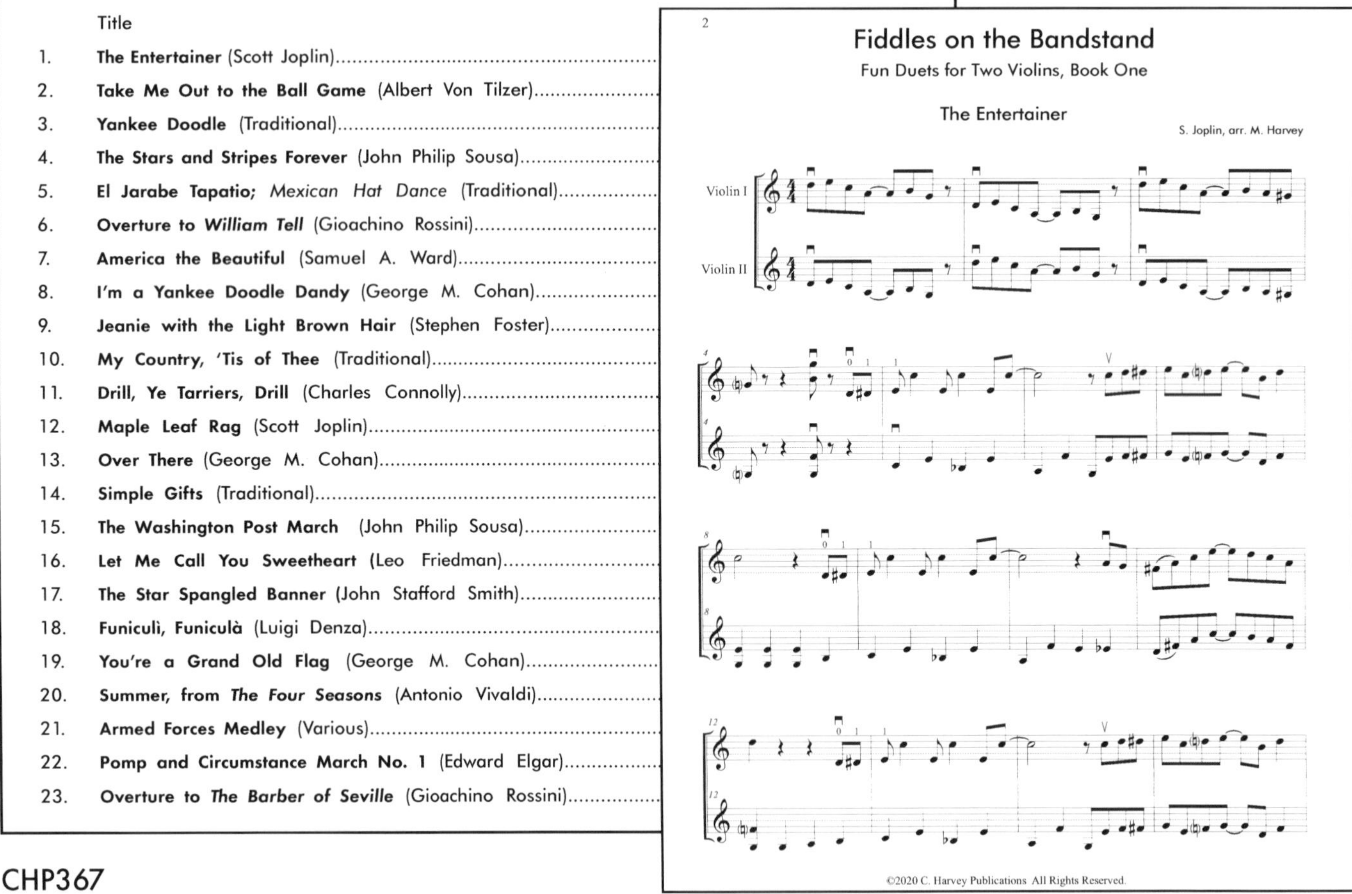

Title

1. **The Entertainer** (Scott Joplin)....................
2. **Take Me Out to the Ball Game** (Albert Von Tilzer)....................
3. **Yankee Doodle** (Traditional)....................
4. **The Stars and Stripes Forever** (John Philip Sousa)....................
5. **El Jarabe Tapatio;** *Mexican Hat Dance* (Traditional)....................
6. **Overture to *William Tell*** (Gioachino Rossini)....................
7. **America the Beautiful** (Samuel A. Ward)....................
8. **I'm a Yankee Doodle Dandy** (George M. Cohan)....................
9. **Jeanie with the Light Brown Hair** (Stephen Foster)....................
10. **My Country, 'Tis of Thee** (Traditional)....................
11. **Drill, Ye Tarriers, Drill** (Charles Connolly)....................
12. **Maple Leaf Rag** (Scott Joplin)....................
13. **Over There** (George M. Cohan)....................
14. **Simple Gifts** (Traditional)....................
15. **The Washington Post March** (John Philip Sousa)....................
16. **Let Me Call You Sweetheart** (Leo Friedman)....................
17. **The Star Spangled Banner** (John Stafford Smith)....................
18. **Funiculì, Funiculà** (Luigi Denza)....................
19. **You're a Grand Old Flag** (George M. Cohan)....................
20. **Summer, from *The Four Seasons*** (Antonio Vivaldi)....................
21. **Armed Forces Medley** (Various)....................
22. **Pomp and Circumstance March No. 1** (Edward Elgar)....................
23. **Overture to *The Barber of Seville*** (Gioachino Rossini)....................

2

Fiddles on the Bandstand

Fun Duets for Two Violins, Book One

The Entertainer

S. Joplin, arr. M. Harvey

CHP367

$9.95 www.charveypublications.com

Take a journey to a simpler time when lawn chairs and blankets would be out under the stars and music would waft out from under the eaves of the wooden bandstand.

These are the tunes that got our feet moving, made us smile, and brought us together. Now, with these violin duets, you can bring the toe-tapping, exuberant joy to others and remind us all that through highs and lows, music can be something we share to keep our spirits up and build community.

From Scott Joplin to John Philip Sousa, these violin duets will invite you up on the bandstand, out for a gig, or out on your lawn to play your heart out! Know any violists or cellists? You can pick up a copy of the viola or cello book and play with those instruments as well; the violin book is fully compatible with the viola and cello books.

This violin book is mostly in first position, with occasional basic third position.

Made in the USA
Columbia, SC
07 June 2025

59065608R00028